MYSTERIES OF SCIENCE

HAUNTED HOUSES

THE UNSOLVED MYSTERY

BY LISA WADE McCORMICK

Reading Consultant:
Barbara J. Fox
Reading Specialist
North Carolina State University

Content Consultant:
Andrew Nichols, PhD
Executive Director
American Institute of Parapsychology
Gainesville, Florida

Capstone
press®

Mankato, Minnesota

Blazers is published by Capstone Press,
151 Good Counsel Drive, P.O. Box 669, Mankato, Minnesota 56002.
www.capstonepress.com

Books published by Capstone Press are manufactured with paper
containing at least 10 percent post-consumer waste.

Library of Congress Cataloging-in-Publication Data
McCormick, Lisa Wade, 1961–
    Haunted houses : the unsolved mystery / by Lisa Wade McCormick.
    p. cm. — (Blazers. Mysteries of science)
    Summary: "Presents the mystery of haunted houses, including current theories
and famous examples" — Provided by publisher.
    Includes bibliographical references and index.
    ISBN: 978-1-4296-3394-9 (library binding)
    1. Haunted houses — Juvenile literature. I. Title. II. Series.
BF1475.M33 2010
133..1'22 — dc22   2009005056

Editorial Credits
Katy Kudela, editor; Alison Thiele, set designer; Heidi Thompson, book designer;
    Svetlana Zhurkin, media researcher

Photo Credits
Alamy/Dale O'Dell, 13, 24; Greg Vaughn, 8–9
AP Images/The Hutchinson News, Lindsey Bauman, 18–19
Courtesy Save Our Heritage Organisation, 6–7
Fortean Picture Library, 12, 26–27
Getty Images/Hulton Archive/FPG, 25; Time Life Pictures/Ed Clark, 10–11
Landov/Reuters/Jessica Rinaldi, 22–23
andé Lollis, 4–5
Shutterstock/Arlene Jean Gee, 14–15; Drobova, (image bullets) 16–17; Elixirpix,
    cover; Marilyn Volan, grunge background (throughout); Maugli, 16–17
    (background); Michael Effler, 20–21; rgbspace, (paper art element) 3, 17;

TABLE OF CONTENTS

CHAPTERS

A Scary House 4

What are Haunted Houses? 10

Studying Haunted Houses 18

Haunted Findings 24

FEATURES

Famous Haunted Houses 16

Glossary 30

Read More 31

Internet Sites 31

Index 32

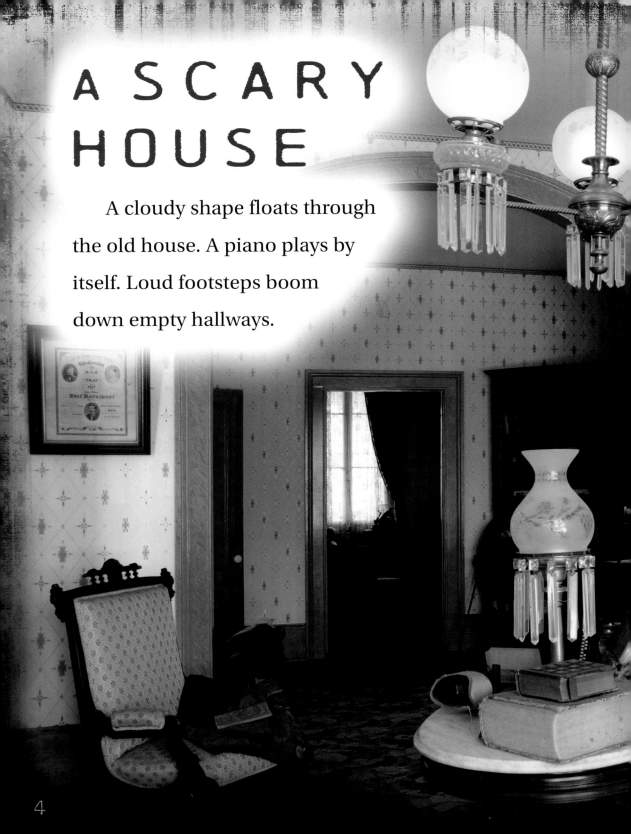

A SCARY HOUSE

A cloudy shape floats through the old house. A piano plays by itself. Loud footsteps boom down empty hallways.

The Whaley House in San Diego, California, is a scary place. People claim they have seen **ghosts** there. Others have heard the sounds of children crying.

ghost — a spirit of a dead person

6

Built in 1857, the Whaley House has a spooky history. The owners often heard footsteps in empty rooms.

Today the Whaley House is a museum.

Could the Whaley House be **haunted**? Some people say it is the most haunted house in the United States.

haunted — having strange events happen often, possibly due to ghosts

WHAT ARE HAUNTED HOUSES?

Strange events happen in haunted houses. Some people hear screams. Others see lights turn on and off by themselves.

HAUNTED FACT

One of the earliest ghost stories comes from Ancient Greece. In this story, a ghost in chains walks through a house at night.

People say the ghost of "The Brown Lady" haunts England's Raynham Hall.

Haunted houses often have a spooky past. People died or were killed in these houses. Some say the ghosts of those who died stayed in these buildings.

Most haunted houses are old.
But some new homes are said to be
haunted. Some haunted houses are
near battlefields or **graveyards**.

graveyard — a piece of land where dead people are buried

HAUNTED FACT

Ghosts don't just haunt houses. People say they have seen ghosts in castles, hotels, and other buildings.

FAMOUS HAUNTED HOUSES

A ghost wearing a green head scarf appears at the Myrtles Plantation. Some visitors to this Louisiana house have seen handprints in a mirror. Other visitors have heard footsteps on the stairs.

People say the ghosts of slaves haunt the Lalaurie Mansion in New Orleans. Visitors to this home claim they have heard moans. They say ghostly faces have appeared in windows.

Six family members died at the Stranahan House in Florida. People believe the ghosts of these family members now haunt this home. Some people have smelled perfume. Others have felt a cold hand on their backs.

People say they have seen ghosts at the Winchester Mystery House in California. Visitors claim they have heard footsteps and banging doors. Many say they have seen the ghost of former owner Sarah Winchester.

STUDYING HAUNTED HOUSES

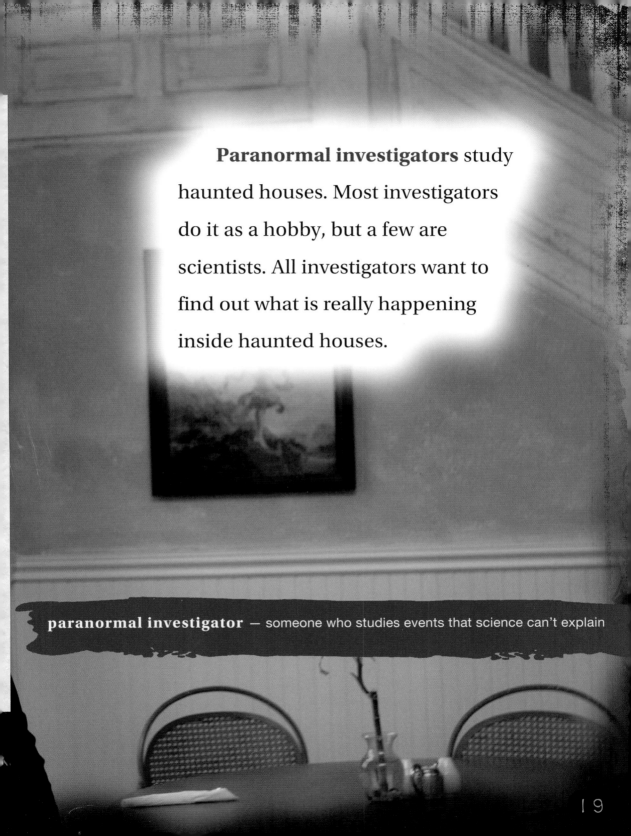

Paranormal investigators study haunted houses. Most investigators do it as a hobby, but a few are scientists. All investigators want to find out what is really happening inside haunted houses.

paranormal investigator — someone who studies events that science can't explain

Investigators find many causes for spooky noises. Tree branches can bang against windows. Squirrels in an attic make a lot of noise.

HAUNTED FACT

In 1991, a New York court ruled that a house in Nyack, New York, was haunted.

Paranormal investigators often spend the night in haunted houses. They set up cameras to take pictures of ghosts. Many also record strange noises or changes in the temperature.

Investigators say the temperature can drop 10 degrees Fahrenheit (5.5 to 5.6 degrees Celsius) when a ghost is in the room.

HAUNTED FINDINGS

Scientists say there is no **proof** that houses are haunted. They say many ghost pictures are not real. Some people have even **faked** hauntings at their homes.

proof — facts or evidence that something is true

fake — to pretend that something is real

Paranormal investigators say their pictures are real. They believe houses and other buildings can be haunted. They say science can't explain all the scary events.

Is this ghost real? Experts do not know if this photo taken at Newby Church in England is real or fake.

What do you think? Are some houses haunted? The answer is still a **mystery**.

HAUNTED FACT

Some haunted houses have odd smells. Many believe these smells are from ghosts.

mystery— something that is hard to explain or understand

GLOSSARY

fake (FAYK) — to pretend that something is real

ghost (GOHST) — a spirit of a dead person believed to haunt people or places

graveyard (GRAYV-yard) — a piece of land where dead people are buried

haunted (HAWN-ted) — having strange events happen often, possibly due to ghosts

mystery (MISS-tur-ee) — something that is hard to explain or understand

paranormal investigator (pa-ruh-NOR-muhl in-VESS-tuh-gate-ur) — someone who studies events that science can't explain

proof (PROOF) — facts or evidence that something is true

READ MORE

Krohn, Katherine E. *Haunted Houses.* The Unexplained. Mankato, Minn.: 2006.

Oxlade, Chris. *The Mystery of Haunted Houses.* Can Science Solve? Chicago: Heinemann Library, 2006.

Williams, Dinah. *Haunted Houses.* Scary Places. New York: Bearport, 2008.

INTERNET SITES

FactHound offers a safe, fun way to find Internet sites related to this book. All of the sites on FactHound have been researched by our staff.

Here's all you do:

Visit *www.facthound.com*

FactHound will fetch the best sites for you!

INDEX

battlefields, 14

castles, 15

deaths, 13

footsteps, 4, 7, 16, 17

ghosts, 4, 6, 10, 13, 15, 16, 17, 22, 23, 28
graveyards, 14

hotels, 15

Lalaurie Mansion, 16

Myrtles Plantation, 16

noises, 4, 17, 21, 22

paranormal investigators, 19, 21, 22, 26
pictures, 22, 24, 26

scientists, 19, 24
smells, 17, 28
Stranahan House, 17

temperature, 22, 23

voices, 6, 10, 16

Whaley House, 6, 7, 9
Winchester Mystery House, 17